WE NOT ME

Serving Generous Families
with an Ensemble Enterprise

John Moore

Renown
PUBLISHING
WRITE YOUR BOOK & REDEEM CULTURE

To Connie—
wife, lover, mother, business partner, travel partner,
Grammy, generosity caper creator, drinking buddy, and
daughter of the King.

CONTENTS

Chapter One 1

Chapter Two.. 13

Chapter Three.. 25

Chapter Four 35

Chapter Five.. 45

Chapter Six... 63

About the Author.. 79

Chapter One

A decade and a half after I'd traded in my Air Force flight suit for a business suit, I'd become accustomed to no one calling me "Colonel" or "Sir" anymore. I was simply John.

Instead of climbing the ladder into cockpits, I was climbing up in the financial services world. Instead of soaring through the clouds at breakneck speed, I spent my days compiling investment strategies and studying tax law and market forecasts. Instead of attending daily briefings, I met with clients and reported to my branch manager.

During the late 1980s and early 1990s, I also linked up with Terry DeLaPorte a few weekends a year to co-teach Christian business classes for Family Life Radio. Terry was a former athlete and coach who had become a business consultant, integrating biblical stewardship principles into the fundamentals of business strategy.

On those weekends, we found ourselves in conference rooms or church halls in Michigan, Arizona, and New Mexico—wherever Family Life Radio broadcasted—speaking in the main sessions of financial advice seminars, then holding breakout sessions, integrating biblical stewardship principles into their business strategy. I tried to get on Terry's travel schedule when we could because he flew with Delta and usually upgraded us to first class with his frequent flier miles. It also gave us time to talk—me from my decade-old perspective as a financial advisor and Terry as a business consultant who had years of experience coaching athletics.

It was the direction my career had taken, which was weighing me down as I stowed my carry-on bag in the overhead compartment and took my seat in the Boeing airliner. Terry sat beside me on this particular flight, one of the few times we traveled together. "What does it mean to truly serve Christ in a business environment directed at profit?" I asked as other passengers continued to shuffle by, eyes searching for their seat assignment.

"That depends. Is your primary obligation to the client or your employer?"

"What do you mean?" I clicked my seatbelt together and tugged the strap. (Much of the following conversation was prompted by self-analysis after reading great books like *Business by the Book* by Larry Burkett and studying business applications in Proverbs, but I've included many of my thoughts in the form of dialogue.)

"As a broker and money manager for Prudential, is your primary obligation to each client or the company?"

"Employees work for their firm." I stuffed my ticket in my seat pocket. "The obligation is to the employers. By doing my job, I help the client."

"But you're asking how to genuinely serve as a Christ follower in your position, right?" Terry asked. "What if it was the other way around? How would your office look if everything you did was for the customer first and the employer second?"

I had to ponder that for a moment. "My office would be a completely different place."

"How long have you been with Prudential?"

"Seven years. Before that, I was with EF Hutton for ten."

"What type of office environment did you have at EF Hutton?"

"They were a very intrapreneurial firm." I smiled, and no, that word isn't spelled wrong. "I had a lot of freedom to build a business model different from anyone else in the office. I never pushed a product at the first meeting. I simply built relationships and asked for an appointment."

"Sounds great."

"I loved it. I developed a twenty-seven-question quiz with yes or no answers. But I wouldn't let clients get away with a simple yes or no. Every question led to a discussion, and I built relationships through that process."

"How did you convert relationships into sales?"

"In follow-up meetings, I came back with a recommended solution and spoke with them as friends." This approach is much more productive and biblical than the typical transactional sale. I learned the question-centric approach at the Dale Carnegie Sales Course and with the Wilson Learning Counselor Salesperson curriculum. I also felt it was biblically solid because it put emphasis on determining clients' needs and providing solutions to address them.

As the aircraft began to back away from the terminal, he turned to me. "How is that different from your role at Prudential?"

I shook my head. "My boss loves to say, 'Have you done your Grover today?'"

Terry chuckled. "Grover Cleveland? The president who quietly reigns on the elusive one thousand dollar bill?"

"He's asking if I made one thousand dollars in daily commission."

"Clever."

"It's clever once. After that, it wears on you. He ranks us based on our production and posts it in the office. Sometimes I'm the hero, sometimes I'm a zero."

"Ouch."

"I'm the highest producer in the office. I've brought in plenty of capital and revenue for the company over a twelve-month period because I manage my book of business well by taking care of the clients." I shrugged. "But the manager hounds me if I haven't dropped tickets for generating commission on any given day."

"That's what I'm talking about." Terry reached for his briefcase. "The workplace culture would be different if your primary obligation were to the client instead of the employer."

"Oh, I always make sure to put the client first." I shrugged. "But with the not-so-subtle pressure they put on us, I'll have to quit if I one day find I can't do that."

"We've got the same issues at my office. It feels very transactional and drives me nuts. In any service industry, we will succeed when we focus first on helping the client." I shook my head as jet engines roared to life, and inertia pressed me into the seatback.

Terry pulled out his notes for the talk he would be giving later in the day and set them on his lap. "I think the disquiet you're feeling is because there's a disconnect in values between what we teach on these trips and what you do every day in the office."

I nodded. "If business had a ministry focus and wasn't there just to make money, I think I'd be in my sweet spot."

"I agree," Terry said. "There's quite a difference between a ministry that helps people prepare their fiscal futures and a financial firm where you're just trying to close a sale."

"What if the two could merge?" I said. "Maybe it's a pipe dream, but I'd love to see an office prioritizing biblical financial principles."

About five hours later, we were teaching workshops on the very principles I longed to see put to work for my clients. As the son of a Baptist pastor, I had trusted in Jesus Christ at a young age. While I wouldn't consider myself a theologian, I read through the Bible from nose to tail every year. My experience in the finance industry dovetailed with Terry's knowledge of theology. Together, we covered a range of financial and leadership topics from a biblical worldview. Since Jesus taught about cultivating a godly mindset toward money more than He did about heaven and hell combined, we did, too. We taught from the heart and loved every minute of it.

During that particular trip with Terry, I imagined what it would look like to truly put the customer first, using tools like the Discovery Sheet questionnaire that I was still using at Prudential and would carry forward to John Moore Associates. We would know every client well, not just their financial picture but their lives—where they came from, their dreams and aspirations—and then customize their financial picture around them. Every client interaction would be more relational, giving the best possible services through good relationships, and we would serve them based on biblical principles. No more striving for Grovers and having purely transactional conversations.

By the time we landed back in Albuquerque, I wondered if it might be possible to begin changing the culture at my office.

Over the next few years, I moved up in my firm despite the counterproductive ranking system. Encouraged by my mentors to make the workspace look first-class, I used my own business account to hire a designer. We turned our office into a showpiece with our unique flair, including a white marble conference table. In addition to the basic computer my company provided, I also built an in-house computer network. That included the Customer Relationship Management (CRM) system, which helped us keep track of our clients' information.

Back home, my wife, Connie, and I were also busy raising two beautiful young daughters. We had upgraded from a modest starter home to a much nicer one on four acres out among the mountains, just a short drive from Albuquerque. We were some of the early llama people in the 1980s. Then, as neighbors moved away, we ended up inheriting their animals: more llamas, big fuzzy rabbits, a pony, and sheep. We had a barnyard full and a stock trailer for when they needed to go for a ride. Taking the animals to our church's living nativity scene at Christmas was always a delight because our llamas often stood in for camels.

One day, I came home from the office and slumped over the kitchen table. Connie rarely saw me like this and was immediately concerned. "What's wrong?" she asked.

"Late last night, someone broke in and stole our entire computer system."

"Oh, my goodness. You spent thousands of dollars on that."

I nodded. "And we invested hundreds of hours of time."

"I'm so sorry," she said. "Did you call the police?"

"Yeah, they came and poked around. When they saw no signs of a break-in, they determined it must have been someone with a key."

"Someone at the firm?"

"That's what they think. The police aren't going to do a thing about it."

"What about your manager?"

"He refused to investigate. Office politics. But it's not just about the computers. It's my client list. Someone from our office is coming after me."

She frowned. "Why would they do that?"

I ran a hand through my hair. "Scarcity."

"What?"

I took a bag of M&Ms from the cupboard, poured them into a bowl, and set it between us. "They think of our city like a jar full of M&Ms. Each represents a potential customer, a limited number." I took out a handful and set them on the table. "If I have more M&Ms than they do, they feel slighted—as if I've done something to them. Then they somehow feel entitled to what I have."

I pushed the bowl aside. "They're stuck in a scarcity mindset, living in their silos and striving for their daily commission run. It appears some of them have targeted the top producers and will do anything they can to take them down." It wasn't until later I learned that over the last few years, sixty people at my production level had been chased off from the firm. It appeared that Prudential as a company was removing top producers to save money on the higher payout rate to those producers.

She put an arm around me and pressed in. "What are you going to do?"

I picked up the Yellow Pages. "First thing in the morning, I'm calling a security firm and having a camera installed."

"What about going out on your own? You've started companies before. I know you could do it again."

"It's not that simple." I sighed. "If they discover I'm leaving, they'll terminate me. It's entirely possible they'd just tell people they don't know what happened to me or why I left. They could even sue, though I don't really expect that to happen."

She looked me in the eye. "What are your options?"

I held Connie's hands. Together, we prayed. We gave the whole situation to God and asked for His wisdom and guidance. The next day, I went back to my office and had a security camera installed, then I bought new computers. I also began conversing with people outside of finance, seeking solid business advice. I once again wondered if operating a financial firm using biblical principles was possible.

That was a moment of truth for me. If I truly wanted to do what I felt God was placing on my heart, I'd need to take that first step, regardless of any fears telling me to keep my head down.

From that day forward, I started putting my ducks in a row to prepare for a move. I started a search for office space to lease or buy but had to do so quietly without letting Prudential get wind of my plans. There was a lawyer I knew who had also gone independent, a friend of mine who I could trust. He gave me solid advice.

"You're tempted to go cheap on space," he said. "Don't. Maintain the high standard your clients are used to. Also, if you plan on keeping any of your current clients, which you can legally do, stay close to your current office. If you move more than a block away, they will think you've moved out of the country."

I kept looking at properties, and Connie and I continued praying diligently about going out on our own. If we were going to do it, we had to know it was God's plan for our lives.

A moment arrived not long after starting JMA that helped confirm our plan had been worth it. I attended a Raymond James Financial conference, joining hundreds of professionals listening to the latest tax law and finance practice updates. This was far more casual than the large firm meetings I'd attended. Guys sat spaced comfortably in business casual—no ties allowed. You could smell the coffee in the air. I sat in the back to observe what was happening and pick out the leaders among them that I should seek to know better later.

I didn't expect much more than, "This is how to make the big bucks for the firm," so I resigned myself to hearing the same. I took out my pen and paper and mulled through my business plan again. Barely listening to the speaker, I wrote at the top of my page, "The client's needs will come first."

Then, I heard the speaker say, "The client's needs will come first."

I looked up. His voice held my attention like a siren's song. Forty-five seconds later, he repeated, "The client's needs will come first."

In my seventeen years in finance, I'd never heard a senior leader discuss this concept. Now, I'd heard it twice within a minute. I made two hash marks on the top of my page. He continued his talk, updating the group on events at the firm, and repeated the line every few minutes. Each time, I made another mark. His emphasis on caring for the client resonated with my soul. I could see how this change would revolution-ize the finance industry. During the forty-five-minute speech, I made fourteen hash marks on my page.

I breathed a sigh of relief. "Thank You, Lord. I might be in the right place."

That relief had taken a long time to appear. I remembered that before JMA could exist and I could recreate the culture I valued, we had needed to take one fateful step.

With the theft and the lack of response from the firm still weighing on me, I left work early and stopped by a real estate firm. I toured an available office space a block away from my current office and signed a lease. Then, I went home and reported everything to Connie.

She took my hands into hers. "How can I help?"

"Remember about a month ago when we ducked into the office after hours to pick up some files?"

"The security guard gave you a hard time."

I nodded. "Let's hook up the stock trailer."

Focused and on mission, with Connie as my wingman, we backed up our stock trailer to the firm's door at midnight. After disarming the security system, we loaded the trailer, which had been swept clean of the manure or hay you might expect to find. One by one, we lumbered out all my personal belongings: computers, chairs, and even my white marble conference table. As we left the office, sweaty and smelling like the back end of a llama, I slid my resignation under the manager's door.

We drove away from the parking lot to an uncertain future. I recruited a small, loyal team from my former employer to join me. Once we had moved into the new space, Connie brought our daughters to visit. They looked out the eighth-floor windows, saw various buildings in the distance, and said, "We can see both malls from here!"

With no salary and a tremendous amount of new expenses, I wondered if they'd be stepping inside a mall at all in the next few years. I gathered the whole group, including Connie and the girls, and we prayed together. We dedicated the office space and our entire new venture to God.

I took out my notepad and envisioned what type of business I wanted:

- The client's needs come first.

- Our office will have a culture of being relational with clients.

- As stewards of the business, we will act like managers, not owners.

- Our guidance and teaching will be unashamedly based on biblical principles.

- No more scarcity mentality. We will live with an abundance mentality.

- God would make the phone ring.

- When I'm looking for the magic word to close the sale, God makes them say yes, not me.

I was back on the phone in no time, smiling and dialing our previous clients. Some of our old clients joined us. Others stayed at the last firm, including my lunch buddy, the lawyer.

Two weeks after we moved in, an envelope with a law firm's name as the return address arrived. My previous employer had filed a lawsuit against me.

Connie looked at me. "Now, what are we going to do?"

Chapter Two

That late-night move was decades after I had first donned my olive-green USAF flight suit—the fighter pilot icon—for the first time during pilot training at Craig Air Force Base in Alabama. The flame-resistant suit, a one-piece design with a front zipper, chest and thigh pockets, and patches, showed off my rank, unit, and other identifiers, proudly displaying my resume on my chest.

My assignment right out of training in 1972 sat me in the front seat of my F-4 fighter as a first lieutenant with the 13th Tactical Fighter Squadron. Since we would be flying in an active combat zone, the rank insignia and unit patches were more subdued, camouflaged against easy identification if we were shot down or had to bail out over enemy territory. My backseater was an experienced Weapons Systems Operator, a WSO or "wizzo" as we called them. We took off with three other planes and flew our designated sortie in formation. I kept a tight line just a few yards from my wingman. About halfway through our flight, I shook the stick side to side and said to my backseater, "You have the aircraft."

"I have the aircraft," he answered.

He wavered side to side, unable to keep a tight formation, and it showed to everyone else on the flight. The moment we landed, the flight leader, a lieutenant colonel, pulled me aside and chewed me out. "That was a sloppy formation. You need to be crisper. This is a combat zone."

I stiffened. "It was my backseater. He's the one who couldn't hold formation."

He looked me in the eye. "Who's the aircraft commander?"

My heart sank as jet engines roared in the background. "Yes, sir."

I respected his authority. He could have crushed my dreams and been harsh with me, a lowly greenhorn. Instead, he was direct and supportive. I looked up to him and respected that he took the time to invest in me. From then on, I was never bashful about providing feedback. If someone needed input, I gave it to them in an effective way, like my squadron leader had for me.

As with most military careers, every eighteen months or so, orders came through for a new assignment, often in another state or country. Early in my career, I was stationed at Udorn Royal Air Base in Thailand. I was still relatively fresh, but the military's strict rules ran through my veins. We had regulations for everything from our uniforms, salutes, and rank to each mission's parameters, especially in the air. We followed protocols for speed and altitude in the presence of small arms fire from the ground to ensure the safety of the pilots, the aircraft, and everyone involved.

We walked a tight line and didn't cross the rules. Discipline reigned supreme.

On one mission, I guided my F-4 Phantom through our scheduled pattern in the mix of other types of aircraft. I followed a major with seniority over me into a high-threat environment. He flew too low and too slow, violating all sorts of principles. In the middle of his foray into a flight without rules, I had to increase my speed to preserve my ability to avoid enemy threats. Sweat soaked my flight suit. My own body odor filled the cockpit. With his variations from our plan, I constantly re-calculated "bingo," the point with the minimum fuel level required to return to base. His plane was burning less fuel than me because he was going slower. I gritted my teeth, held the stick, and kept doing evasive maneuvers to avoid getting shot.

I didn't wait for the alarms to blare. Once I saw my fuel was running low, I got on the radio and called out, "Bingo."

"Return to base," the major responded.

When we landed, I confronted him. "What were you doing flying 250 knots at that altitude? That's far too slow. You should have been pushing 400 knots."

"Why did you go to bingo so fast?" he snapped.

"I had to keep my speed up to avoid potential small arms fire, and that caused me to burn more fuel than we had planned. Plus," I pressed, "I was in the position to be the one who would get shot behind you."

He waved me off without a thought.

I requested that I never fly with him again.

Flying fighters requires absolute confidence in one's abilities, and stereotypes exist for a reason. A cocky fighter pilot exudes self-assurance both in and out of the cockpit with a swagger that comes with being the best in the business. Competitive and attention-seeking, we constantly pushed the envelope in the air. The base was full of these guys, myself included.

Later, I was honored to be selected to attend Fighter Weapons School, the Air Force's version of the Navy Top Gun School. There, I learned more than I could have imagined. The school was about more than just flying an airplane. As a class, we had training on tactics and enemy threats, and they required each of us to give daily briefings. Of course, in the days before PowerPoint, we used overhead projector slides and even had to get a projectionist license. We wrote technical manuals for mission tactics and limitations of the aircraft in specific situations. We also were taught the teaching and coaching skills I would later find valuable in my civilian career.

Being military, nothing but precise wording with correct grammar was acceptable. We also had plenty of time in the air, performing tactical scenarios in air-to-air dog fights, just like in the movie *Top Gun*. Upon graduation, we were fully qualified to be an instructor's instructor. I eagerly accepted my new role and commonly gave talks to sixty or one hundred other pilots from various squadrons in the wing at that base.

It wasn't just flight instruction that kept me in an instructor role, though. Like most young adults, many pilots I interacted with were beginning their careers without knowing anything about managing their finances. They did stupid things with their money, like spend it on fast, expensive cars and burn through it at the bar. Every squadron seemed to have a guy who offered financial advice: how to make a personal budget, how to save, and where to invest for the future.

In our squadron, that guy was me. That part of life came naturally. I met with guys individually, helping them balance their checkbooks, create a budget, and invest wisely. After a while, this became second nature. It was rewarding to watch young couples transform from struggling in debt to living in financial freedom and growing their nest egg as they began families of their own.

Like most of my fellow pilots, I was known to frequent the local bars on a Friday or Saturday night. During one such weekend, I met a young woman named Connie, who was an elementary teacher at a local school. After growing up in Columbus, Ohio, she was looking to get out of town and experience something new. So, she took up the invitation of some friends in the Air Force to take a job in the Southwest, and eventually, we ran into each other. We ended up spending a lot of time together after that, and we eventually got married.

What can I say? Fighter pilots are babe magnets—and they're humble, too. All kidding aside, the truth is that in military terms, I married above my pay grade, and Connie tolerated the fighter pilot idiosyncrasies.

Connie and I enjoyed spending time with the other pilots and their families, especially a couple we knew as Barry and Judy Wade. I instantly saw that Barry was an exception to the stereotype. He served as a flight commander, mentoring a group of eight pilots. He lived simply and honored God to the point of being meek. I'd never seen a fighter pilot without swagger. He became a plumb line for me, a standard for how someone can live for God.

Yes, I'd grown up in the church and had given my heart to Jesus Christ years earlier. However, life as a fighter pilot was filled with enough distractions to keep me centered on myself. It had been a long time since I'd picked up my Bible or spent any time in prayer, but Connie and I admired the Wades and kept an eye on how they lived. In time, the example of how they lived their lives shifted how we lived our lives as well.

It wouldn't be all missions or training duties for me all the time. In 1978, I would be assigned to serve as a demonstration pilot flying the A-10—a single-seat fighter—in air shows at Air Force bases and civilian airfields across the country. I was covering the East Coast while another pilot covered the West Coast. The two of us showed the public what our aircraft was capable of with low-speed passes, high-G turns, aileron rolls, Cuban eights, and simulated close air support. After landing, I'd hang out by the plane in my flight suit, answering questions.

"What's that?" A boy asked after one demonstration, pointing at the business end of the GAU-8 cannon.

"The A-10 is a world-class gun with an airplane built around it," I said with a grin.

"What type of bullets does it shoot?"

I let him hold the foot-long bullet. "We can deliver 4,200 armor-piercing rounds a minute."

Jaws dropped. Eyes widened.

Another boy asked, "Why is it so ugly?"

I motioned to the broad, straight wings and twin engines mounted high on the rear fuselage. "People might call it the 'Warthog,' but you saw it can perform, right? It does the job."

They all smiled. I loved every second of it.

As part of my role as a demonstration pilot, my commanding officer assigned me a secondary task: to meet with the leadership of the Massachusetts Air National Guard and brief them on the benefits of the A-10 that had been recently assigned to their squadron. This was, in effect, my first foray into the world of sales, except I wasn't trying to shepherd investors.

I entered a meeting room in Boston to address the commanders and senior leaders of the Massachusetts Air National Guard and presented my case. After my brief presentation, an official held up a photo of the A-10. "You've got quite an ugly duckling there."

I laughed. "It's not something you take your girlfriend out to see, but this plane can fly circles around the F-100."

He looked through the paperwork. "This thing can get a bird strike from the rear."

The room erupted in laughter.

I nodded. "It's not the quickest plane in the Air Force, but we're talking about protecting our country. Are we interested in having the best-looking plane? Or the fastest? Or do we simply need the machine which can do the job better than anything else?"

He stood up.

I spread my arms. "How would you like to see it in action?"

He looked at his companions, then turned back to me with a smirk. "One against four?"

I nodded.

We took to the skies, me flying the A-10 and them sending up four F-100s at a time. As each flight ran out of gas, I was able to stay airborne for three or four flights against the F-100s. We simulated combat, too, but with a gun camera instead of the real thing.

I smiled as the thrill of the simulated fight coursed through me. About two miles away and two thousand feet above me, one of the F-100s gained altitude for his attack run. I leveraged the A-10's maneuverability and quickly gained a superior position to fire at him with the gun camera, using a devastating attack of my own. Emerging from that skirmish, I pulled back and left on the control stick and rolled into a defensive spiral, enabling me to evade the weapons of the final fighter jet before taking him out as well.

After a morning flight and an afternoon flight, the officials' expressions had changed. Their questions shifted from mockery to strategy and tactics. We talked for a few hours about how and why the Warthog was a true upgrade to their fleet. We wrapped up the day by celebrating long and hard at the squadron bar, capping off the evening with a nice dinner in Boston.

The next morning, I woke up in my hotel room feeling every single drink I'd had the night before. There was still plenty of time before I had to head home, so I turned on the television. Evangelist Robert Schuller was on, and he shared a simple and profound message. I don't remember what

Scripture he quoted, but I remember hearing this: "It's time to come back to Jesus."

When I heard those words, something stirred inside me. I felt God's presence. The Holy Spirit got ahold of me. Jesus's grace, mercy, and love overwhelmed me in that hotel room.

Everything about me faded into the distance. I knew in my heart I'd been focused on the wrong things. My life had all been about me. My performance. My airplane. But now, only God mattered. I fell to my knees and called out for forgiveness. Then, I picked up the hotel Bible and started reading. I don't know how long I stayed there on my knees, but when I stood, I was a different man.

Later in the day, I cranked up the A-10 to head home from Massachusetts to Myrtle Beach, South Carolina. As I passed the Statue of Liberty, shining green in the sunlight, I asked God, "What am I gonna tell Connie?"

The answer was clear. "Just go tell her what you heard."

I walked through our front door and greeted her with a hug. Something in that moment told me she was different, too. I shared with her everything I'd experienced and repeated the words I heard in the hotel room. "It's time to come back to Jesus."

"I'm ready." Connie had tears in her eyes. "God's been working on me, too."

We prayed together and rededicated our lives to Jesus. As we talked, we both realized how much of an influence Barry and Judy Wade had on us as unwitting role models of faith.

Connie and I started reading the Bible together. We developed a habit of daily prayer, both individually and as a couple. We also started attending services at the Air Force base's chapel regularly. I learned priorities and began to shift things. Jesus came first in my life. Connie was second. Work had its place, but it needed to be third. Acclimating to this new way of thinking, I found joy and peace I'd never known.

The military has a habit of changing things up with new orders right when we get comfortable. One of the most coveted jobs in the Air Force is to be an operational test pilot. The adventure of determining weapons' system capabilities and proofing new hardware while sometimes pushing the limits in the latest aircraft means living on the edge.

I wanted that job. The flight suit couldn't talk to me, of course, but if it could, it would have been whispering, "This is it. The next step."

At this point in my career, I'd performed well enough to land an assignment as an operational test pilot, and at the same time, I'd reached the end of my commitment to the military. I had the option of re-upping my commitment or turning it down and leaving the Air Force.

Connie saw my expression when I came home. "What's going on?"

I told her about the assignment. "It comes with a seven-day option to accept or resign from the Air Force."

"Sounds like a career-defining move."

I nodded.

A few months earlier, I wouldn't have given it a second thought. I would have immediately accepted and told Connie we were moving to Nevada. But with Jesus first, I had to ask Him if this was the right move.

Connie and I got in the car and drove around for six hours. There was no radio, no nothing except the hiss of the tires on the pavement and the rumble of the engine. "God, should I take this job?" I prayed. "Are you giving me my heart's desire? Or is this something you're asking me to walk away from?"

I didn't hear an audible voice from God or see the clouds rolling back like a scroll, but by the time I parked my car, I knew in my heart I was not supposed to take the job. At 1500 (3 p.m. civilian time), I walked into the Air Force Personnel Office and turned in my resignation.

Walking out of the office, I symbolically reached my hand out and shook the stick. This was it. A positive change of control is the term we used to denote clearly who is flying the plane. "Okay, God, You have the aircraft."

Chapter Three

That was 1980. After leaving active duty in Myrtle Beach, South Carolina, I was offered a position as an A-7D pilot with the New Mexico Air National Guard. I kept my civilian pilot's license active. I needed to find a full-time career since Guard service was part-time. I felt a clear calling to utilize my avocation of providing financial advice as my new vocation while keeping aviation as an avocation.

Thankfully, God had a path prepared, as I hoped He would.

One of the commanders in our Air National Guard unit was friends with the branch manager at EF Hutton in Albuquerque. He offered to make an introduction. I accepted the gracious offer and, a few days later, found myself sitting for an interview with his friend, Dave Browning, Branch Manager, at EF Hutton's Albuquerque office.

After a quick discussion about their office and services, Dave cleared his throat. "John, this is a sales job. What makes you think you'll be a good salesman?"

I pulled out a postcard with a picture of the A-10 and handed it to him. "Dave, is this not the ugliest airplane you've ever seen?"

He recoiled. "Not much of a looker. Why are you showing me this?"

"I did much more than fly jets in the Air Force." I pointed at the photo. "Part of my job was to convince federal officials of the significant capabilities of the Warthog as a needed alternative to their sleeker, faster jets."

"Tough sell."

"This is the best machine for support against tanks."

"Were you successful?"

"The Air Force bought a fleet of these multi-million-dollar aircraft. In addition to the active duty units flying the A-10, it has assigned them to Air National Guard units in several states other than New Mexico. They function much like the Enchilada Air Force unit—also known as the Tacos—here in Albuquerque. Not too long ago, I was able to demonstrate the A-10's capabilities to the Massachusetts Air National Guard and convince them it was indeed an upgrade to their existing supersonic, swept-wing F-100 Super Sabres. These aircraft will be around for a long time."

He picked up the photo. "If you sold this monstrosity, I suppose you can sell just about anything."

"Put me in, coach. I'm ready to play."

He set the photo down. "Tell me about your team."

"We say we in the New Mexico Air National Guard are the second-best group of pilots in the world." I grinned. "That being said, we haven't met the first-best yet."

He chuckled. "How about the rest of the team?"

"What do you mean?"

He raised his palms. "Who packed your parachute? Who did the maintenance on your aircraft?"

"Oh, yeah. We had a solid team through and through."

"You were a high-ranking officer. When you walked into a room, everyone stood up. You gave the orders, right?

I shrugged. "I had a lot of years on the stick."

"You might find civilian life a bit different from your previous world. Everyone from the mailroom to the boardroom has an important role."

"Of course."

He continued. "When you walk into a room, nobody will stand up. Giving orders has a different feel, and they may not be followed to the letter just because you said so."

I bit my tongue. "No problem."

Dave gave me a desk in the bullpen and a nominal base salary for one year. After that, I'd be on 100 percent commission, so it was incumbent on me to generate a list of prospective clients. I had to be the very definition of a self-starter.

Dave taught me how to build a book of business, a career. As a forward-thinking leader, he saw that women serve women much better than men. At that time, a woman in the industry was unheard of. He hired Carol Jones, who became the first female branch manager in the country. He brought in a number of people outside the finance world, taking a risk on a boot salesman and even a fighter pilot.

It didn't take long to figure out how their system worked. I took courses and learned how to make the magic close and get the client to say yes. I absorbed every inch of the business. Though it felt transactional, like a business deal without meaning beyond the handshake, I began to thrive in their system. After a few months, I felt like I was hitting my stride. I'd met everyone in the office and developed working relationships all around. I had a new swagger in the world of finance.

Meanwhile, I was thoroughly enjoying my service as a member of the New Mexico Air National Guard. Pilots were my people. We had everything in common, and I enjoyed spending time with them and their wives or girlfriends while staying in touch with our friends from active duty, especially Barry and Judy. We enjoyed sharing our freshly renewed faith with them.

But pilots tended to stay away from doctors. They provided a service we felt we didn't need and, more importantly, held the power to ground us. I only visited a doctor when I had to complete my annual physical required to serve as an Air Force pilot. In addition to annual physical exams, the Air Force used periodic check rides to provide rigorous accountability to ensure proficiency and safety.

I was scheduled for a visit with the flight surgeon after my Instrument Proficiency Check. I concluded a scheduled check ride in my A-7, performing every aspect of the flight to perfection. I strutted across the street to the doctor's office, smelling like exhaust fumes. I exchanged my flight suit for an embarrassing hospital gown, which opened in the back. Talk about humbling. The doctor looked me over and found nothing wrong. Since I'd reached the age of thirty-five, he ordered an EKG. A tech attached twelve wires to me, and a machine drew lines on paper. After he left, I jumped up, donned my olive-green status symbol, and waited in the sterile white room. When the doctor walked in, I jumped up and said, "See you next time, Doc."

"Not so fast. Have a seat." His face was full of concern.

"What's wrong? Everything is fine, right?"

He showed me a page full of squiggly lines. "These heartbeats are normal, but look at this." He pointed at a wide squiggle. "This is a premature ventricular contraction."

"Okay, so?"

"One of these now and then is fine. Two is a concern. Three in a row is considered tachycardia."

I had learned a new term. Hearing it was like being punched in the gut. Tachycardia equaled no more flying.

He pointed at a specific spot on the page with three closely linked blips in a row. "We're gonna need you to do a stress test with your civilian doctor."

My jaw dropped. "Doc, are you taking away my wings?"

I had to come to grips with the idea that I might have just taken my last flight in the Air Force.

This couldn't be happening.

I glanced down at my flight suit. My whole identity was wrapped up in that baggy olive-green outfit. It was practically reaching toward me. I shook my head. Without it, who was I?

I'd shaken the stick and given God the controls, but it didn't seem right. In the cockpit, I was the best of the best, 450 knots at one hundred feet, flying with precision. I gave the orders Monday through Friday and made the magic happen in the air. But on Sunday morning, I wore church clothes and tried to look and act the way people expected a Christian to be. I lived with a disconnect between Sunday and Monday.

But clipping my wings? Grounding me? What was God doing?

I would soon discover, though, that He had a new, better future in mind for me, though not without important lessons I needed to learn.

One of those lessons occurred several years into this new career when my assistant took another position in the company, and I acclimated to working with a new young lady. Then, about a year later, she moved on as well. It didn't take me long to go through three sales assistants. Nobody seemed to be up to snuff.

One of my associates had an all-star assistant named Karen. She managed most of her boss's duties, leaving him to focus on closing clients. His sales numbers were through the roof. Karen interacted with plenty of people in the office, and she seemed to boost the performance of everyone in her sphere of influence.

One morning, when I noticed she was having a little turbulence with her boss, I approached her. "Karen, what would it take for you to consider becoming my assistant?"

She squared up to me. "There's one person in this office I would never work for, and that's you." Then she stalked off.

The rest of the office heard the comment. With my heart racing and my face flushed, I stumbled back to my desk. I couldn't believe what I had just heard.

That night, as Connie served dinner, I told her about my interaction with Karen.

"So, she knows you pretty well," Connie said.

"What are you talking about? I'm not an ogre."

She took a bite of her meal. "No, John, but you are a military officer at heart. You give orders. Other people follow."

"I just want to be productive."

She looked at me. "Didn't Karen make her point? How do you engage with your assistants?"

"I tell them what I need done. They do it." I pushed a piece of food around my plate.

"I know you don't mean to be harsh, but how you communicate is a little off-putting."

"What are you getting at?"

She sipped her water. "How many assistants have you gone through since you've been there?"

"That doesn't mean—"

"It's not them, John."

I dropped my fork. "Are you saying I'm destined to be one of the worst managers in the history of business?"

She set her cup down. "Tomorrow, watch every interaction between people in the office. Take note of how they speak to each other. You're not in the Air Force anymore."

I had no response. We ate the rest of the meal in silence.

Back at the office, I got up out of my chair and made good on my word, heading out into the bullpen from my private office and covertly—I hoped—observing every word spoken in the bullpen. My office neighbor approached his assistant with a stack of papers. "I can't get all this done, and I'm on a deadline. Can you help me and submit it by the end of the day?"

She flipped through the pages. "I hope so. It might be tomorrow. Is that alright?"

31

"Great." He grinned. "As soon as you can, thanks."

I cringed as I imagined how I would have phrased his words.

The next evening, as I set the table, Connie prepared our meal. I shared the whole exchange with her.

She brought a pitcher of water to the table. "What they lacked in crisp military communication, they made up for in relationships. They were real with one another."

I crossed my arms. "I'm real with people."

She headed back to the counter. "He was vulnerable with her."

I leaned against the kitchen table. "In the military, the only time we used the word vulnerable was when we talked about the enemy."

Connie smirked. "How does the word vulnerable apply in a finance office in Albuquerque?"

I thought for a moment. "Showing where I need help."

"Vulnerability is rewarded with better relationships. Relationships lead to increased productivity."

I took a deep breath. "That's not possible in an office setting."

"Nonsense, your relationships at the office are just as important as our marriage is."

"You mean I should treat them like a marriage?"

"You should work on those relationships just as much as we work on our marriage, sixty-forty."

When we married years earlier, we defined the sixty-forty split as each partner being willing to give more than they take without keeping score. The joy in our relationship thrives on unselfish love and is worth the effort.

"So, you're saying I should strive to contribute a greater share to the relationship than I receive?" I asked.

She nodded. "Exceed expectations."

Over the next few months, I took a file to the harsh edges of my communication and treated people in the office like family members rather than subordinates. They had to be fellow pilots, squadron mates, the ones on whom I relied to watch my six. I tempered my requests, asked questions, and showed where I needed help. My soft underbelly exposed, I gave up on giving orders and held meaningful conversations.

My assistant and I formed a healthy team. In time, my production rose. A few years later, she told me she and her husband were leaving town. As I began planning her going away party, I put out word that I needed a replacement.

Karen volunteered.

I worked with her for the next seventeen years. She even followed me not just to Prudential but out the door when we left to start JMA, remaining an integral part of our tight-knit team.

Chapter Four

After Connie and I backed up our trailer and moved out in the middle of the night, we were off on a new adventure. Connie held the lawsuit in her hands and shook her head. "Now, what are we going to do?"

I digested page after page. They accused me of everything from breach of contract to misappropriation of trade secrets to fiduciary duty violations. In total, they levied forty-seven substantial allegations against me.

I held Connie close. "These accusations won't hold up in arbitration. I know our rights and obligations from our contract. We followed them to a tee."

"It looks serious. Are you sure?"

I couldn't answer.

I looked up the number for my lawyer, Marty. He came by our fledgling JMA office for a consultation right away. Connie, Karen (my superstar assistant), and I sat around on the handful of chairs that were available—we were still awaiting the delivery of the rest of our furniture. The bulk of our records were still stacked in boxes around the room.

Marty flipped through the pages of the lawsuit. His expression grew somber with each turn. "These allegations are precise and go back years. They want to shut you down."

"How hard will it be to combat this?" I asked.

"Fighting this will take a ton of effort." He pointed a finger at me. "You'll need to do some digging to get the appropriate paperwork to show you were in compliance with each client."

My heart sank. "I don't know how we can do that."

Karen went to one of the boxes and pulled out a thick three-ring binder as nonchalantly as if she were reaching for a tissue. It landed on the table with a thud. "This should be everything you need."

Marty's eyes grew wide. "What do you have in there?"

"Every i has been dotted, and every t crossed." Karen smiled.

Marty shook his head. "Nobody is that organized." As he looked through Karen's pages, a smile crept across his face. "This will take some time, but it looks like we've got the ammunition we need."

Meanwhile, we concentrated on creating a professional office environment. Our space had way too much room. I hoped we could someday grow into it. With the extra space, we were able to set up a meeting room that would seat twenty people. Then we found a great deal on gently used but very nice meeting room chairs. The wife of a client, an excellent interior designer, worked with us to create a welcoming reception area and place artwork while selecting office furniture to complement the furniture we brought with us from Prudential, giving the office a professional flair. Connie did everything from buying Kleenex to calling clients. In time, she became known as the "office mom."

Through much prayer and with the help of some trusted advisors, I was confident God was in control of the fledgling John Moore Associates, but as I looked through my financial obligations and what little money we had coming in, I cringed. "If all else fails, I guess I can go back to work somewhere else."

We knew what kind of firm we would build: a culture where we were relational with clients and their needs came first. We would help people be good stewards of God's finances guided by biblical principles. In a battle against the scarcity mindset, we pushed forward with an abundance mentality. God made the phone ring. When we talked with clients trying to close a sale, we trusted Him to inspire their yes instead of looking for the magic word.

A recruiter from Raymond James had given me some advice prior to our big move. "Within a year of starting your new firm, you should have 100 percent of the assets you had when you left your previous job," he explained.

I counted off fifty-two weeks, marked the calendar, and kept close track of our progress.

With our playbook in hand, we got busy smiling and dialing. In the days before SEO and slick online marketing, we just made phone calls and talked to people hour after hour. We spoke to anyone and everyone and never badmouthed our previous firm. Many of our prior clients came to join us. We grinned as we chatted on the phone, laughed at each other's jokes, and occasionally performed what we called the "Dance of Joy" reserved for when a family decides to do business with us.

During an early phone call, one client was intrigued by what he'd heard about us. "I'd like to see your new office," he said.

"We'd love for you to come by," I said. "I'll set something up and let you know."

I immediately approached Karen and asked if she could organize an open house. I wanted everyone to see that we weren't running our new business out of a ramshackle house. She set up a relaxed, informal time for people to hang out in the new space—and as for the date, what better spot on the calendar than around the Fourth of July 1997? We rounded up hot dogs and apple pie. Our Independence Day theme was consistent with our breaking out independently when we left the previous brokerage firm.

Visitors showed up all afternoon. We welcomed familiar faces and got to see a lot of new ones. It was a time of celebration as we enjoyed one another's company. Most of our visitors were CPAs and existing clients, and many soon became great referral sources. About sixty people visited, so many that we ran out of hot dogs. I knew Connie hated spending money on a party, but for building our clientele and showing our friendly faces to the community, it was smart money well spent.

During those first few months, we used our round conference table to meet with clients in the office as often as possible. I made an effort to get to know each of them. One of my early meetings was with a young businessman we'll call Gary, who came in with his wife, who we'll call Melissa. They were Christians with a solid biblical foundation, but regarding his finances, Gary held his money tightly and seemed reluctant to invest or exercise generosity.

In my previous firm, I would have done a risk tolerance assessment and leaned into the benefits of our products. Instead, I pivoted the conversation in an entirely different direction. "Gary, who owns the money in your bank account?"

He quickly responded. "I do."

"What's your goal with your finances?"

"Hang on to it and build a nest egg."

I pulled a fancy black fountain pen from my pocket and held it in my open palm. "Montblanc pens are luxury writing instruments, crafted with meticulous attention to detail with high quality."

I handed it to Gary. He noted the elegant, timeless design. "Is that real gold inlay?"

I smiled as I took it back. "Yes, it is." Then I clenched the pen in my fist. "Try to take it from me."

He looked at me curiously.

"Go ahead."

He reached for it but pulled back empty-handed.

"If I'm holding the pen this way and God wants to take it from me, it's either gonna hurt my hand or break the pen."

His eyes darted side to side.

Next, I pulled a matching pencil from my pocket. "Together, this set costs over $1,000. If God wants to give you a pencil to go with that amazing pen, and your hand is still wrapped tight, there's no way you'll get the additional blessing."

He pursed his lips. Melissa gently held his hand.

I held the pen properly and drew a line on a piece of paper. "How we hold our resources is important. God has given you money in your bank for you to steward. When I gave my life to Jesus, I gave Him everything: my life, my relationships, my career, and even my finances. He gives me work to do and has tasked me with managing the money in my bank account. The money in my bank account is actually His. I'm just a steward. As I care for His money, I need to hold it properly. Sometimes, He increases the blessing."

Gary and Melissa asked lots of questions, and we continued our conversation. Before long, we worked out a viable plan for them.

As our client base grew, our lawyer, Marty, continued to call with updates on the lawsuit. He worked down the list of accusations one at a time. He reviewed the specifics of the first allegation and walked through the legal standards. I shared what really happened, and he verified it with our documentation. The allegation wouldn't hold up. Over and over again, we repeated this painstaking process.

Marty was good at his job, a strategic thinker, and a true counselor. We flew A-7s together in the Air National Guard, and I wouldn't want to go to war without him. But dealing with the lawsuit weighed heavily on me. Even when he's a friend, it's never a good thing when your lawyer's number is on speed dial. Every hour we talked to Marty was an hour we weren't talking with clients or doing anything to help build the business.

In my personal quiet time with God, I cried out to Him for help. I fasted and poured out my heart, pleading for a quick resolution. During that time, I read through the book of Psalms. My heart resonated with the words on the page.

Arise, LORD, in your anger; rise up against the rage of my enemies. Awake, my God; decree justice.

—Psalm 7:6 NIV

I felt like David as I fell on my face before the throne of God, asking the almighty God to protect me from an assault from an enemy. While I didn't write songs about it or even play a musical instrument (other than the sousaphone, which is a terrible instrument for this type of thing), I cried out every day, asking God to rise up against my enemies.

Would He be able to make this thing go away? Do we have enough documentation to cover every charge? If this lawsuit takes me down, what will happen to my team?

I continued meeting with Marty. Slowly but surely, he made progress. Many months into our new venture, he and I wound up on a conference call in my office. The opposing counsel was on the other line. I could hear what sounded like a horse whinnying.

"Where is she?" I whispered to Marty.

"At a horse show in Scottsdale." Marty shrugged, then cleared his throat. "So, what is it you're offering?"

"I'm proposing that the process be concluded with no further action, no arbitration hearing, and no request for reimbursement of legal expenses by either party," he said.

I couldn't believe what I was hearing. *Could it really be the answer we've been hoping for?* A Bible passage came to mind—Matthew 5:25, which says in part, "Come to terms quickly with your accuser while you are going with him to court" (ESV).

Marty raised an eyebrow. "What do you think?"

"We need to put this behind us," I told him. "Let's accept."

"Pending receipt and review of the settlement agreement, we should clarify," Marty added.

He passed along the details to the opposing counsel, and soon enough, the settlement was in place. A weight lifted from my shoulders. "Thank You, God!"

After twenty-five thousand dollars in legal expenses, endless stress, and many sleepless nights, it was finally over.

I could breathe again.

I announced the news to the whole office. They celebrated with an impromptu party.

At home that night, after the kids went to bed, Connie and I sat on the couch. I sighed. "I didn't do anything wrong, and they attacked me. But thanks to Karen's meticulous record-keeping and Marty's work, it's finally over."

She put her arm around me. "You've been justified."

I nodded. "I knew when we started this business, it would be hard, but I didn't know it would be this hard."

"I think God has given us a signal that we were on the right track. He is so kind to us."

Some scars from the lawsuit remain. More than twenty-five years later, when I read the book of Psalms, I'm physically taken back to the stress my body had when we were working through that lawsuit.

We continued reaching out to clients. Fifty-three weeks after we started JMA, we were back to 100 percent of the client assets I had when I left. The recruiter from Raymond James was only off by one week.

JMA was going to be successful.

"I heard from our friend, Marta Kramer, about a trip to Israel sponsored by a church in Chandler, AZ, and hosted by Scott and Laura Brewster," Connie said to me one afternoon. "I'd love to bring the girls."

"I'll give them a call." Internally, I cringed, knowing the price would still be beyond our reach, but still eager to take our family on what could be the pilgrimage of a lifetime.

One phone call later, I was elated. When someone hosts a trip to Israel, they get to go for free. But Scott and Laura decided to pay their way, which allowed everyone else's rates to go down. Their generosity allowed us to go at a significantly reduced rate.

We enjoyed walking in Jesus's steps. One Bible story after the next came to life in the context of their culture and geography. I sat down with Scott and John Kramer, Marta's husband, for lunch in a pizza parlor in Old Jerusalem. I had informally advised them while they were negotiating a contract between the Southwest Airlines Pilots' Association and Southwest Airlines a few years earlier. The company was offering stock options, and I was able to educate the two of them to help them function effectively as members of SWAPA's negotiating committee. Throughout the trip, they had been asking me financial planning questions, and we enjoyed a little shop talk with our pizza.

"How would you design a non-qualified plan for highly paid employees to invest in excess of the 401k limits?" he asked.

I jumped into planning mode and walked them through a couple of creative ideas. John and Scott nodded, listening intently as they ate their slice, and I filled up the silence. "Great," he finally said. "You're hired."

"For what?" I had no idea I was in the middle of an interview.

"We're trying to develop that kind of plan to implement at the company (SWA). We'll hire you to help us find the right consultant."

When we returned home, I met with their group. After a few detailed discussions, they decided that of all the finance guys they had talked to, I was the most qualified. They hired JMA to consult on supplemental retirement plans for the pilots' union. This led to us getting hired to assist employee groups at Southwest, American, and JetBlue. Then, since I knew the SWA benefits package like the back of my hand, I had the perfect platform to market directly to the SWA pilots. I enjoyed talking flying lingo with them and always remembered to wear my pilot's watch. Soon, more than our fair share of Southwest retirees became clients.

With JMA serving our clients from a biblical worldview, I was excited to see what would happen when we were firing on all cylinders. Exciting days were ahead.

Chapter Five

As JMA began to gain a solid footing, Family Life Radio continued to invite me to teach biblical stewardship. I envisioned a written version of the material as a study guide for churches as I walked through my curriculum dozens of times. When our family went to Padre Island for Christmas in 1997, I stayed up late each night and got up early, typing away. I don't know what inspired me, but I wrote the entire manuscript in a week. In 1998, Family Life Radio printed the material as *The Almighty and the Dollar*. They also increased my on-air presence.

I didn't set out with big publishing plans. I simply honored my commitment to teaching biblical wisdom.

Connie and I were part of a small group Bible study led by Virgil Dugan at Hoffmantown Church, a large church in Albuquerque. Virgil had two PhDs and had worked for many years at Sandia National Labs. As part of our conversations in the late 1990s, Virgil mentioned he had been working on a quantitative model to calculate company valuations as reflected by the stock market. He noted that he had the math figured out and asked if I could help him with the "common sense" application of the calculations. This model became a foundational part of the JMA investment process, and Virgil has been engaged with JMA since then.

When the leadership team at Hoffmantown learned about *The Almighty* book, I was asked if I could teach a four-week series through the book. They consolidated all their Sunday school classes, and we had a giant Sunday school class where I taught biblical financial principles. The church took our chapter titled "Slaying the Dead Dragon" and turned it into a publicity poster with a dragon burning up dollars.

The exposure from these activities helped launch JMA to an entirely different level. Instead of smiling and dialing potential clients, JMA's phone kept ringing. As our client list grew, I didn't have the time or capacity to care for all my clients single-handedly. Peter Lehrman, a friend and colleague, joined our team. He was a bright gentleman with all the proper credentials: Chartered Financial Analyst (CFA) and Certified Financial Planner (CFP). Then Dave Stephens joined JMA, followed a short time later by Jami Schwalm. Together, they helped build our team around the motto, "We, not me."

We challenged each team member to recognize the client by voice, not just by seeing their name on their caller ID. They should have a genuine relationship with them. We also coached each team member to work together as an ensemble. I knew I would return almost all the issues to them anyway, so I empowered them to get to know our clients and take care of them on the firm's behalf. Those relationships would, in turn, benefit the firm and add to JMA's growth.

The goal was "We, not me."

A time came when it seemed appropriate for Peter to leave JMA to start his own business. I consulted with Marty and prayed about the relevant biblical principles before deciding the best course of action for the clients involved. We would let the clients choose if they would go with Peter or stay with JMA. We had in mind Deuteronomy 15:13–15, which states, "When you release a male servant, do not send him away empty-handed. Give him a generous farewell gift from your flock, your threshing floor, and your winepress. Share with him some of the bounty with which the LORD your God has blessed you. Remember that you were once slaves in the land of Egypt and the LORD your God redeemed you! That is why I am giving you this command" (NLT). Now, of course, Peter was no slave, but the command from God about how to treat a worker with respect and dignity was clear.

Through this process, Peter was able to have a sustainable business model from the start, and God provided additional assets to replace the accounts that had followed Peter from our firm. It was a risk we were willing to take to trust in God for the benefit of our business and our clients.

With a firm commitment to guiding our clients in biblical wisdom, I also made sure our advisors were not trying to be prophets. Our clients always want us to predict the markets, like we have any inside knowledge of what will happen tomorrow. The biblical penalty for prophecy going wrong is death by stoning, and I'm not interested.

In addition to stock market predictions, there is also a temptation to predict tax law changes. Some advisors make portfolio adjustments based on proposed changes. I refused.

"Here at JMA, we're not interested in being stoned if we get things wrong," I said. "When a client presses us for an answer, we just tell them we don't know the future but build plans based on conservative assumptions and make adjustments as congressional or regulatory proposals are finalized."

In 2008, our clients watched their hard-earned money dwindle as the market crashed. The S&P 500 fell by approximately 57 percent from its peak in October 2007 to its trough in March 2009. I held more one-on-one meetings during those gloomy years than at any other time in my career.

I met with one of our long-time clients—we will call him Larry. As we looked over a dismal earnings sheet, he scowled. "John, let's get out of the market."

"Larry, you're a business owner, a fixer. When something's not working in your business, you try to fix and improve it. Right?"

"Absolutely. What can I do about this?"

"The best thing to do right now is stay the course. Don't do anything. Simply let the market correct itself. You're going to be fine."

He was visibly shaking. "How can you say that?"

I pointed to a photo of an airplane on the wall. "Did you know I used to fly in the Air Force?"

"No."

"When you're flying a high-performance airplane, if the airplane goes out of control, normally the best thing you can do is let go of the controls. As long as you have plenty of altitude and your aircraft is structurally intact, you'll be okay."

He rubbed his eyes. "How does that work?"

"In the late 1940s, during the early days of supersonic flight, the planes lost control unexpectedly and tumbled end over end. Some inexperienced pilots would have ejected, resulting in a complete loss of the aircraft and danger to themselves, but Chuck Yeager was the best. While he cartwheeled in his airplane, forty thousand feet above the earth, he just sat there waiting it out, not even grabbing the stick. Eventually, the pointy end goes into the wind, air moves over the wings again, and you have lift. All it needs is time, and the plane will fly itself out."

He motioned with his hand like a plane going down. "We're certainly in trouble right now."

"You're forty-five years old. Your portfolio is well-positioned. You have plenty of time for this thing to come back. This is not the time to panic."

He nodded.

I pressed the issue. "In fact, if you have any money saved, this would be a great time to put more into long-term investments."

He raised his eyebrows.

"Right now, everything is on sale. Connie likes to say, 'The only thing people don't want to buy when they're on sale is stocks.' With history on our side, the markets will likely recover, and we don't want to miss the recovery. I'm sure Chuck Yeager might have had his hand on the ejection handle, but he wisely did not pull that handle and didn't miss the recovery to controlled flight."

He took a few deep breaths. "Fine."

Since financial stewardship dovetails with our spiritual life, our clients' meetings often drifted into spiritual conversations. In time, our meetings with clients became a discipleship ministry. I encouraged all team members to actively disciple their clients and help them grow in their relationship with Jesus.

Discipleship is a long-term process. We don't expect each client to go from being an agnostic to turning them into Billy Graham overnight. We just take them one step at a time. If they are at level two in their spiritual life and just figuring out how to live like Jesus, we talk about moving to level three. Sometimes, I ended a meeting with a new client by saying, "I don't know if you're the praying kind, but I'd like to put you on our prayer list." I was continually surprised when some of the harshest people responded, "That would be great."

Throughout my career, I attended training events by Ron Blue and other Christian financial leaders. The Christian Financial Professionals Network (CFPN)—now known as Kingdom Advisors—was an excellent resource for networking with and learning from other like-minded financial planners. At one of the conferences, Ron told a story about a journey he and his family took on vacation and some fantastic sights. The expedition leader knew the local terrain, where to stop and rest, and where to press through. Without a professional guide, they would have gotten lost and had a terrible experience.

"You are the guide." He paused and looked around the room. "You can't take your clients where you haven't been yourself. If you teach generosity, you must walk in a generous lifestyle yourself."

I had invested well. I'd followed all the basic financial principles. But as a financial guide, I had plenty to learn in the area of giving. I asked God to provide me with opportunities to be generous.

During my early days in business, I put my private pilot's license to good use, flying to see clients and attend board meetings for Family Life Radio. Sadly, I was no longer flying with my hair on fire at 450 knots at treetop level, dogfighting, and dropping bombs, but at least I was in the air.

I kept my hand in the civilian aviation world, flying several different light airplanes. In 1990, we bought into a partnership that had purchased a 1968 Beechcraft Bonanza V35A, the Harley Davidson of light airplanes. We improved the engine with turbo-normalizing. It was fast, about 190 miles an hour. It was a great airplane. While you wouldn't want to take this high-performance V-tail aircraft to the heavy weather on the East Coast, it's hard to beat it for everyday use in the Southwest. It felt like a family member over the thirty years we owned the plane. It was a great way to scratch my flying itch.

A lot of mission organizations use small aircraft for transport. We'd been in contact with a mission organization in Papua New Guinea, where a German World War Two fighter ace served as the air medevac provider. They were the only organization with airplanes equipped to carry patients from the remote islands to the main hospital at the capital. Their crucial mission was lifesaving for the islanders. I was excited to hear what they were doing but hadn't gotten involved significantly yet.

Late at night, as I read a pilot's magazine, an advertisement for a new technology called LORAN got my attention. A company had adapted naval long-range navigation technology to airplanes. I thought about the most challenging mission facing the ministry in Papua New Guinea. The government had constructed an airstrip on one side of a remote island. They could fly out there, but they had no precise means of navigation. When clouds are in the area, losing your way over the vast ocean was easy. Because the island was at the extreme end of the range capability of the aircraft, there would only be a few minutes to spot the runway before the plane would have to turn around and return to its departure point. LORAN might be their solution.

As I tossed the magazine on my bedside table, I heard God say, "Contact the missionary pilot in Papua New Guinea. See if they need a LORAN box for their airplanes."

I learned long ago that when God tells you to do something, don't delay. Do it right away. So, I sent him a letter (this was before email). Sure enough, he had heard of it and knew it would be a tremendous help, but the expensive technology wasn't in their budget.

Connie and I discussed how the LORAN technology would make a massive difference for them. We bought one and sent it to them right away. My heart filled with joy, not only because we had done a good deed but also because this gift dovetailed with my passion for flying, and I knew God had sparked the idea. My passion was now serving God instead of me being in servitude to my passion.

A short time later, the missionary came to visit us in Albuquerque... "You must have been listening to God because we needed this badly." We continued to interface with this ministry for several years.

God dropped opportunities like this in our laps time and time again. Either I saw a need, or Connie did, and we embraced opportunities to be generous. As we exercised our generosity muscle, our giving became more effective.

Our client list continued to grow. We served a lot of middle-class folks as well as a select few high earners. Scott and Kay were our most prominent clients at the time. We managed their portfolio and enjoyed a healthy relationship. As like-minded Christians with similar value systems and a great sense of humor, they were a joy to be with.

At one of our regular meetings, Scott announced, "John and Connie, we would like you to come on a cruise with us."

I was shocked. "Seriously?"

"We're heading on a fifty-foot sailboat for ten days."

I held up my hand. "I'm sorry, Scott. We have a rule that we cannot travel with clients."

He shook his head and chuckled. "Then we're gonna fire you because we want to be your friend."

I changed our policy on the spot.

Sometimes, sharing a story of generosity is precisely what people need to hear to take the challenge of growing in their relationship with God through giving. While on this sailboat charter, Connie and I shared some of our stories, which opened the door for discussions about giving from an abundance mentality, giving from your first fruits rather than your leftovers. We talked about giving where your passion lies and getting the best bang for your buck. We discussed building a giving portfolio of organizations in which we could invest for the long term. Our conversations even turned to when declaring your gift as a public endorsement of an organization can be helpful and when it's better to remain anonymous. Generosity is a complicated business.

When we returned home, I looked over our client list. So many of them were great friends. "Why do the big companies make policies that do not emphasize being friends with clients?"

"It's much harder this way," Connie said.

"What do you mean?"

"I'm on the phone all day. I love chatting with everyone. It's business, and it's personal."

I beamed with pride. "You've embodied our company's mission."

"I tell clients our story and discover their families' struggles, but I can't let my hair down and have to be careful to represent JMA professionally. I need to be on my A-game all the time."

I held her hands. "You are a great office mom."

She squeezed my fingers.

"The big firms separate business from personal relationships to keep it simple," I told her. "But we're not doing that. God is the one who makes the business happen, not you, not me."

"Clients sense it. They like our atmosphere and know we're not holding things lightly."

"You remember the Johnsons?"

She smiled. "I'm so impressed with those guys. They've built several businesses and sold them for a profit."

"Have you heard what they are doing now?"

"Another new startup?"

"This one has all the markers of success." I rubbed my finger and thumb together. "If it's okay with you, I'd like to put some of our personal investment dollars into their business."

"Thanks for asking. I trust you. Go ahead." She smiled.

"It feels like our family is growing."

"What do you mean?"

"Most of our clients are friends." I smiled back. "Many are so close that I think of them as family."

We continued our client appreciation hot dog adventure every year. It soon grew beyond what we could host in the office, and we moved the event to a baseball stadium with a nice picnic area where we could share a meal while enjoying the baseball game. Clients loved it, and many look forward to our event every year. We emphasize the "bring your friend" mentality. Many clients bring their grandkids along. Over the years, we've held all kinds of client appreciation events, and our clients love them. But we've learned that even though marketing is important, God is the one who makes the phone ring.

One day, the front desk person buzzed my office and indicated there was someone on the line who was asking about becoming a client.

I took the call and came on the line, introducing myself and asking, "How can I help you?"

There was a pause for what seemed like too long. A woman's voice said, "I'm an openly lesbian Jewish rabbi. Will you take me as a client?"

The explanation threw me off for about half a second. "It's nice to speak with you. Well, as a quick and direct answer to your question, we may be on the quintessential opposite side of some issues, but why don't you come in for a visit, and let's discuss what we can do."

A few days later, we sat together at the conference table in my office, and I gave my regular introductory discussion, concluding with how JMA is all about applying biblical wisdom in the advice we give our clients. At the time, we were using different investing language. If that conversation were today, I would have said to her, "We use four words to describe five uses of money: Live, Give, Owe, and Grow. Live is your lifestyle, or what it costs to be you. Give could be support for your church or other causes you care about, including family. Owe actually represents two uses: debt and taxes. Grow is what you do with what's left. Everyone's pie is a different size, but it only has four slices. Each slice impacts the other. For example, the giving slice impacts the tax slice."

After a few more questions, the rabbi, who I will call "Sarah" in the context of this story, said, "It's about time my portfolio had some biblical wisdom applied to it."

It wasn't long before she and her partner signed on as our clients. A few years later, she returned with an even more pressing issue—her congregation was suffering a financial crisis.

"We're in quite a situation here," Sarah told me. "I don't know how we're going to make it through."

"I think what we need to start off addressing is extended generosity. I have always thought of the Old Testament as more rules-based, but there are several examples of generosity in those Scriptures," I said by way of introduction. I reviewed with her the story of the Bible's first fundraising campaign when Moses asked for money for the tabernacle in Exodus 25. We discussed how Moses cast a clear vision for the people before making his ask. Then, the people gave exorbitantly. In Chapter 36, verse 6, Moses said, "Men and women, don't prepare any more gifts for the sanctuary. We have enough! So, the people stopped bringing their sacred offerings." Their contributions exceeded what was needed to complete the whole project.

Sarah shook her head. "I wish we had to tell people to stop giving. It's quite the opposite."

"Let me share another story." I leaned forward. "A rabbi at the back of a synagogue watched people put their offerings into the collection box. The rich people dropped their gifts in the box, and a poor widow came by and dropped in two small coins. The rabbi said, 'This poor widow has given more than all the rest. For they have given a tiny part of their surplus, but she, poor as she is, has given everything she has.'"

"Profound."

I motioned with my hands. "When we give, we draw closer to God, and He honors even the smallest gift."

"I'm not familiar with your story. Where is it from?"

I smiled. "It's from the New Testament, Luke 21."

She nodded. "There's plenty of wisdom in those words."

"How would you like to bring your congregation's leaders in for some in-depth training on generosity?"

She nodded again, her expression grave. "I think that would be helpful."

I was given the opportunity to share with these leaders the principles of biblical stewardship and generosity. They asked good questions and began to apply the principles. Over the next few months, their conversations about finances changed, and a generous gift of $100,000 saved their synagogue's financial situation.

Over time, I shared much about my life and family with Sarah. I told her about my mother, who was living in an assisted living facility where my sister worked as the building director. In the spring of each year, my sister would organize a "senior" prom for all the residents. She would invite the local service clubs who visited her building to come and be the "prom dates" for the residents. They dressed up, set up lights and music from their era, and held a serious party. They all loved it. Three weeks later, my mother passed. It was a classic graduation story—a senior prom followed by graduation. (I like to refer to the passing of a Christian as graduating instead of dying.)

As I shared this, Sarah's tender heart popped out. She gently asked some questions and listened while I talked about my mom. She helped me start the process of dealing with grief.

Later, I realized she had stepped into pastor mode when she saw my need.

Our relationship with this person of Jewish heritage was a gift. We enjoyed sharing our story and faith with someone we would never have expected to be receptive. Of course, I never would have expected to benefit from pastoral care from an openly lesbian Jewish rabbi.

As JMA grew into a mature organization, I wondered which direction God would take us as we headed toward finalizing a succession plan. As Terry DeLaPorte would say, "There is no success without succession."

The idea of legacy really hit home when I attended a 2006 conference hosted by the Raymond James Chairman's Council, an entity whose membership is limited to just a few of their best advisors. These are individuals who excel at taking care of their clients and demonstrating fiduciary integrity.

We were ensconced in one of the primary meeting rooms at the Ritz-Carlton Hotel in Chicago, just twenty or so of us from around the country. This was the first year for the Chairman's Council retreat, but I had looked forward to it with great expectations based on the agenda that included time with top executives, such as the CEO of Raymond James himself, who were part of the panel.

One of the most anticipated sessions involved a man named Mark Tibergien, who had worked for a CPA firm specializing in serving financial planning institutions and later became Chief Executive Officer of Pershing Advisor Solutions LLC.

"I'm not here to try to sell you on anything," he said from the front of the room. A PowerPoint presentation glowed on the screen behind him. He gestured at the words emblazoned up there. "But to tell you it's important to consider whether you want to have a practice or an enterprise."

I jotted notes as I listened. The words were familiar, but I wasn't sure exactly where he was going with this. Other financial advisors in the room gave each other curious looks.

"I'm trying to show you how to create value," Mark continued. "If your career is just about you, that's fine. You want to make a good living, have great clients, be friends with them, and support yourself and your family. Those are laudable goals."

He raised a finger. "But what if you want to build something that outlasts you? What if you want to build something someone would want to buy? If that's the case, you have to plan for an enterprise rather than a practice. You have to have enterprise. So, the question to consider is, are you creating value for yourself in the future and for your family?"

You can think of the difference this way: a practice would be a financial planner who has a successful business making enough money managing fifty to one hundred clients, with a couple of employees, with the rest left over after payroll, expenses, and taxes as the advisor's salary. With an enterprise, though, the advisor would cap his or her salary at a certain amount, and then once expenses and taxes were paid, the remainder would be reinvested in the firm. This reinvestment could be anything from updated technology to new furniture to rebranding efforts or even a new building.

I remember gently slapping my hand to my forehead. *Why didn't I think of this? More importantly, why am I not doing this?* I jotted down more notes, especially when Mark mentioned the book he had written on that very topic, *Practice Made Perfect: The Discipline of Business Management for Financial Advisers*. We each received a copy of the book before we left the conference.

By the time I returned home, I had read it cover to cover and found that one of the appendices would give our accountant, Rob, step-by-step instructions on how to set up exactly what I wanted to do. A lot of it had to do with organizing tax filings properly according to the IRS guidelines.

I made a copy of that page and handed it over to Rob, our accountant. "This is what we're doing from now on."

He gave it a quick look and nodded. "Okay." Just like that.

It was an exciting change, one that had me hopeful for the future of JMA as we built an enterprise that would outlast me.

Chapter Six

In the days before Zoom calls, I held one-hour in-person meetings, beginning in the afternoon after a business lunch. As soon as I wrapped up with one client, another sat down. Connie called it "The John Moore revolving door." I'd jot down a few notes and jump on a phone call between meetings if lucky. If I didn't have time, the notes and calls piled up for the end of the day. As the founder and CEO of JMA, it felt natural to run at this crazy pace, but I never expected any of my team members to replicate the revolving door.

JMA was honored in the *Barron's* magazine list as the number one ranked advisor in New Mexico for ten years in a row. That got the phone to ring. In 2014, a representative from the Raymond James public relations department called. "You better be on your best behavior. An editor from *Barron's* will be calling you for an interview."

The next day, a guy with a thick New York accent called. "*Barron's* does these stories to highlight top advisors. Tell me your story."

"It all starts with understanding that God owns everything. We are just His stewards." I talked through the biblical wisdom I shared with every client. Then I said, "Since we've started keeping track in 2012, our clients have cumulatively given away over thirteen million dollars."

"It's nice that your clients are philanthropic." His condescending tone was unmistakable. "When clients give their money away, the value of their portfolio decreases. How would your story motivate another financial advisor to follow your example?"

I cleared my throat. "Since we've been keeping track and celebrating giving with our clients, our assets under management have seen a net increase of approximately seventy million dollars."

I heard him frantically taking notes. *That certainly got his attention.* "We encourage all our clients to have a giving plan. After keeping track for a few years, we've found that people with a plan end up giving approximately 30 percent more than those without one."

In our short interview, I poured out as much biblical wisdom as I could muster. The article in *Barron's* was a feather in our cap. We've used total client giving as a metric since 2012. The next day, I realized I had miscalculated the increased assets.

It was actually one hundred seventy million dollars.

As we emphasized generosity with all our clients, many of them asked for specific opportunities for them to get involved. I shared some organizations Connie and I had vetted and were passionate about. But when the same request came in repeatedly, we decided to use our annual investor education day meetings for our clients to highlight a different ministry or charity each year. JMA encouraged client generosity by offering matching gifts.

After one of these annual events, Connie and I looked through our giving portfolio. "These organizations are in almost every continent," I said.

"What if there's a mission opportunity right around the corner?" she asked.

I thought back to my childhood. "I have a personal history with the Zuni people."

"Well, that sounds like the perfect connection." I graduated from high school in the small town of Gallup, New Mexico, just a few miles from a Native American people group called the Zuni. My father was a pastor, and when my parents divorced, his church fired him. At that time, no churches would hire a divorced pastor. But when the Zuni mission lost their pastor, the denomination waived their "no divorcee" rule in desperation, and Dad served as their pastor. The community stayed isolated, rarely accepting outsiders. With my dad's continual presence there, we made inroads into the community. As a teenager, I worked as a DJ at a local radio station in Gallup. Ever since then, I've loved the Zuni people.

I mentioned the Zuni connection to my friend, Virgil Dugan, from Hoffmantown. Virgil was familiar with the mission work in Zuni and offered to accompany us with his wife, Sandy, on a visit to the reservation. With generosity in our hearts and Virgil's encouragement, Connie and I visited the Zuni reservation, looking for service opportunities. While most of the towns in New Mexico have grown and modernized since my high school days, Zuni looked pretty much the same: dirt roads and old, run-down buildings. The dry, dusty smell was even the same as it had been forty years before.

We had the privilege of spending part of our morning touring the Zuni Christian Mission School, which has roots in the Pueblo clear back to 1897. Our host explained how they emphasized Zuni culture along with Christian teaching. As a former teacher, Connie's love for children showed through. When I saw the passion in her eyes, I knew we would be helping.

In 2010, the Zuni Christian Mission School started a fundraising campaign to rebuild the entire campus. At first, donations came in like lone tumbleweeds in the desert. Virgil Dugan was familiar with one of the Michigan-based key funders of the project and informed us that they would be willing to provide more funding if more local businesses and individuals joined the effort. We joined the effort and spread the news about their need for finances. Then, as local businesses, churches, and individuals partnered, resources continued to flow, and the final building—a new combined gym and ministry facility—was completed and dedicated in 2017. As we celebrated at the dedication of the facility, it was clear that God was at work in the middle of the Zuni Pueblo.

During the COVID pandemic, the community naturally self-isolated. The school parking lot became an internet cafe for the pueblo, with free wi-fi available in the parking lot. Connie and I felt led to cover one month of the school year's tuition for all the children to assist the school and relieve some financial burdens experienced by the families involved.

The parents and children sent many letters and cards thanking us for our support.

We invited representatives from the Zuni Mission to be the featured ministry at our next client event and celebrated the story of a Zuni Tribal Police officer who was a leader in the church that is co-located with the school and also a parent of children who attended there. Our clients were inspired by the story and provided additional generous financial support for the school.

Watching others embrace the gospel and share their love through joyful giving was one of the highlights of my career.

As a way to encourage charitable giving in response to the COVID pandemic, the IRS allowed people to deduct 100 percent of their adjusted gross income. At JMA, we decided to leverage this new rule and up the ante in every generosity conversation with our clients. We explained that the IRS had given us a once-in-a-lifetime opportunity and asked, "What kind of gift would be a game-changer for you?"

Several of our clients took that conversation to heart with impressive responses. When I asked one lady the question, she sat still for a long time. Her husband had been tragically injured in a car accident and ended up taking his own life. Also, her son struggled with mental health issues and had been in and out of rehab for years.

"Take some time," I said. "Pray about it. See what ideas God gives you."

A few weeks later, she returned. "I've been discussing this with the women in both of my Bible study groups. I want to make a game-changer gift of one million dollars."

I took out my paper and pen. "Fantastic. Where will it be going?"

"The short-term rehab programs haven't helped my son."

"I'm so sorry," I said.

"But I have a vision of a village of tiny houses. A rehabilitation center for young men learning to be independent where they would stay for six to twelve months, not just a few weeks. They would encourage one another, learn new skills, and be accountable."

I could envision the cluster of small homes packed together into a cozy neighborhood, with people lending a hand to whoever was in need. "This is a wonderful idea."

She shook her head. "But a million dollars won't even buy the land."

I raised my eyebrows. "I can see you've done your homework."

A tear ran down her cheek. "Can you help me make this vision come true?"

"Absolutely. Let me make some calls."

I contacted Al Mueller, a colleague of mine who helps connect people to non-profit organizations, and shared the widow's story. He was quiet for a moment. Instead of jumping into options of where to give the money, he shared a parallel story of a friend of his involving suicide, drugs, and PTSD. Then he said, "I'll help you find a place for that money, and I'm not going to charge for my services."

Al did some digging and found a non-profit organization I'd never heard of. They had a drug rehab ministry with an excellent track record operating in Central Phoenix. They

CHAPTER SIX

had an empty lot adjoining their current facility. In addition,
they already identified a surplus manufactured home suitable
for their site for approximately $100,000.

We visited the organization with the widow. She asked a
lot of questions about the treatment program and its history.
We toured the existing facility and explored the adjoining lot.
When she saw the possibilities, she clapped her hands together in joy. "This will be perfect."

With Al's help, a gifting strategy was designed and imple-
mented. A few months later, the organization scheduled a
ceremony to dedicate their new buildings. The widow recruited the folks from both of her Bible study groups to come
with her. JMA rented a bus and brought the whole group to
the celebration.

The joy on her face when she talked about this experience
was fantastic. There's no way to explain it.

These instances of radical generosity were what I wanted
to see JMA continue even after I retired. The process of selecting a successor and transitioning that successor into the
primary leadership role had begun many years before.

I had met with my attorney, Marty, and discussed typical
ongoing issues in our firm. Then he turned to me and said,
"You've got more salt than pepper in your hair these days.
Tell me about your succession plan."

I ran a hand through my snow-white hair. "You mean retirement? I figure I'll spend more time with my grandchildren."

"I mean a succession plan for JMA, your baby. You need to start looking for someone to spearhead it as a new CEO."

"My baby." I took a deep breath. "I hope they turn it into a one-hundred-year company."

"What would that look like?" He picked up his pen to take notes.

I steepled my fingers. "If I had my way, I'd want JMA to continue with the values and vision that's in place. Certainly, the processes will change with the technology, but not the values or culture we've built."

"Keep that culture flowing?"

I nodded. "Don't forget about Tina, though."

Our daughter, Tina Deshayes, had been working with us for several years. Everyone assumed Tina would be the succession plan for JMA.

"Remember when Connie and I were returning from Phoenix with Tina and her husband, Jason?" I asked Marty. "We heard a voice from the backseat say, 'One small business succession plan is enough risk for one family. Don't count on Tina being your successor.' This was referring to the fact that Jason was a partner in a local CPA firm and was the presumed successor there. While Connie and I were disappointed in this news, we were also thankful that they had communicated their plans so that we could pursue an alternative plan."

Marty put his pen down. "Thanks for that reminder. I've been thinking about finding a JMA successor for a while. I believe I specifically know what kind of person to look for, a leader who embodies your culture."

In May 2013, Marty sent me an email encouraging me to meet with a young man named Brian Cochran. He and his wife, Emily, attended the same church Connie and I did. Brian stuck out in the crowd as a tall, good-looking thirty-year-old former all-state high school quarterback for the state of Washington. He was with Thrivent Financial, a financial organization founded by Lutherans, and was considering going out independently as an advisor. Working at Thrivent, I suspected that Brian thought of me as a competitor. But Marty's endorsement spoke volumes.

We met for breakfast and enjoyed a little small talk. "What's the most important part of your practice?" I asked.

"It's not enough just to know your clients," he said. "I strive to build relationships with them. We need to actively do things with them as much as possible."

"How do you do that?" I asked.

"Our work with Habitat for Humanity and Roadrunner Food Bank have been great partnerships—organizing food drives, providing volunteers, and the like."

Brian and I ordered breakfast, and he continued, "We do activities with our friends and value them as people. Then, when we meet for work, we stay in that relational mode. When 80 percent of a client meeting is talking about family, and only 20 percent is portfolio, that's when it really starts to be fun."

Between bites, we dove into the weeds of business and discussed practical ways to apply a biblical worldview to financial planning. I was surprised at how well-aligned we were. We talked about everything under the sun and had a great time together. If we both hadn't had obligations elsewhere, we'd still be having breakfast right now.

Brian contacted Marty to review his agreement with Thrivent and explore the possibility of going out as an independent advisor. We continued having conversations about our values, looking at how each of us got things done and why we did what we did. When there was a disconnect or any rub, we talked it through, got to the source of the disconnect, and discovered how truly aligned we were. The more we talked, the more it became apparent that Brian would be a good fit, not just as an addition to JMA but as a potential successor to the CEO position.

Over the next few months, we imagined what a succession could look like. I spoke with colleagues who had been through the process and heard their stories of wins and losses. In my seventeen years of experience on the Family Life Radio board, I'd gotten to know the founder, Warren Bolthouse, very well. He built the radio network from scratch and surrounded himself with great staff and a strong board. Warren's leadership was steadfast and committed to a biblical standard. I was involved with seamlessly transferring his leadership to his son-in-law, Randy Carlson. That ministry is still thriving as Randy has handed the leadership to his son, Evan.

Brian and I ended up writing a book on succession planning. It was actually two books, with one written from the predecessor's perspective and the other from the successor's perspective. We included questions at the end of each chapter to help facilitate conversations. We saw how Moses transferred his authority to Joshua, and Paul handed his baton to Timothy. Each situation had unique challenges. We were dealing with a unique business model and a significant age gap between the two of us.

It's challenging for the predecessor to let go of his baby. He holds it close and doesn't want to give it up. He knows the best thing to do is to hand over the reins but often can't bring himself to let go. Many financial firms have had succession plans fail. When disharmony is evident in a firm, clients leave, destroying the baby in the process. Those who failed had one thing in common: they didn't write out their expectations. If the predecessor didn't clearly say what he had in mind, the successor wouldn't know if he was hitting the target.

I was not going to let that happen to John Moore Associates.

Together, we wrote out a clear, step-by-step, three-generation continuity plan and documented it with a letter of intent. The first two years were cohabitation, and we would constantly communicate. He had specific responsibilities. I had others. His role would increase. Mine would decrease. After that, we would move forward with shareholder status and a planned hand-off over the following eight years. If the two-year time frame didn't work out and we had to separate, each client would determine who they stayed with. The clients weren't Brian's or mine. They didn't belong to Ramond James or JMA. They were God's. We tried to create an atmosphere where Brian didn't have to worry about working for two years to build something and leave empty-handed, and I didn't have to worry about losing my baby. We printed off the agreement, signed it, and stuck to it.

When Brian came on board, I stopped thinking, "Is he the right person?" Instead, I intentionally thought, "I can't wait to see what God has in store for JMA." This built a foundation for how the entire office looked to him for leadership. He immediately filled his schedule with one-hour rotating door appointments like mine. He is the only person I've seen who has worked as hard as me. He acted like a founder, not a follower, with an ownership mentality. The company bought him a BMW with a phone in it. He programmed the number one button to speed dial his wife, Emily, and number two for me. He called me every day to debrief. This tight communication either brings you really close together or miles apart.

As part of that communication, Brian and I had discussed the steps I'd already taken to shepherd JMA's conversion into an enterprise model from a practice. When Brian came on board, we continued that work by creating a salary pool. We set it up so that 65 percent would go to me and 35 percent to Brian, which eventually shifted to 50-50 and then more to Brian as I gave up more responsibilities.

"How else should we reinvest in the firm?" Brian asked. We were seated in my office, mulling over ways we should spend the profits that were meant for that purpose.

I drummed my fingers on the arms of my chair. The sound reminded me that the chair was a few years old, at that age where it becomes even more comfortable to sit in because of the way it conformed to the body. "Furnishings, for one. But I don't like the idea of scrambling for the money when we find ourselves in need of making large purchases. The same goes for computer equipment, which is more likely to just fail rather than wear out."

Brian nodded. "It would be good for efforts like rebranding, too—advertising, logos, and the like. So, you're saying we should set money aside for those long-term, planned expenses?"

"A savings account. Taking out a loan is out of the question. We should be earning interest, not paying it."

"Agreed."

That was one of the ways in which we continued to look forward. When we hit JMA's twentieth anniversary in 2017, we created a key theme: "It's not about the last twenty; it's about the next twenty."

This attitude became the prime driver behind the major rebranding effort that I had been dragging my feet on because it was a major expense in the six-figure range.

We connected with McKee Wallwork, an Albuquerque firm that serves big companies worldwide—global but local. They took us through a nine-month process, interviewing key leaders in the company and speaking with clients, and what they heard consistently was one word that would guide them through the rest of the process: "Servants." That was how people viewed us. I couldn't have been prouder.

In the end, the McKee Wallwork representatives rolled out a sheet of canvas that had to be forty feet long, covered with notes, recommendations, and even ideas for logo redesign and marketing themes. But I had one major question for them that I hoped they would answer: "Should we keep my name on the door as I prepared for a time when I would eventually step away?"

What they came back with was brilliant. "Keep the name," they told us. "It's a brand of its own here in Albuquerque that's been around for a long time and garnered lots of exposure. But it's really about a team, not about you. You should leave the name on the door but drop the ampersand."

It made sense. We used to be John Moore & Associates. We became John Moore Associates.

We, not me.

I found Brian giving solid biblical advice to his clients day after day. When I noticed he could improve his language, he soaked up my coaching like a sponge. One day, he mentioned that he was noticing clients were reluctant to leave after their allotted sixty minutes. They needed more time with their complex situations. We switched to ninety-minute meetings and immediately saw improvement in his client's satisfaction.

At our office meetings, Brian displayed tremendous leadership skills. I took a back seat and enjoyed the ride. At first, whenever he made a change, the staff looked at me for approval. I simply motioned back to Brian. Soon, they were fully following him.

Watching another person care for my baby was a new skill I had to develop. I forced myself to let him lead. We talked behind the scenes, but he was the leader in the office. I quoted John 3:30 over and over in my head: "He must increase; I must decrease" (BSB).

Connie visited the office less often, another planned aspect of our succession plan. I reported everything to her day by day. Eventually, I concluded, "Brian is a great thinker with tremendous leadership skills. It's obvious this is the way to go."

"Is it time?" Connie asked.

"I think so."

"Congratulations. How are you going to make the separation?"

I tapped my chin. "I think I need to get far enough away that it's hard for everyone at the office to get a hold of me."

"How about another trip? You've always wanted to visit the great barrier reef," she smiled.

"Let's cut the cord."

We took a marvelous six-week trip to New Zealand, Australia, Chile, and Antarctica. When we got home, I checked in with everyone at the office. It was great to see my friends again. While chatting with them, I was impressed by how JMA was better than before I left.

Around 2016, I made a visit to a doctor at the Mayo Clinic. I pulled open the door and was struck by the sharp bite of medical-grade cleansers. The neutral-colored walls were intended to calm patients as they waited for potentially life-changing news.

I took a seat on one of their ergonomic chairs with vinyl coverings and waited for my turn. As I continued to dream about JMA's new culture, I saw a plaque that said, "The patient's needs will come first."

It hit me like a ton of bricks. Mayo Clinic is one of the most successful medical providers in the country. The simple declaration on the plaque was comforting confirmation that what we had sought to improve by founding JMA was the right course.

Several years later, at JMA's annual Christmas party, I chatted with the wife of an employee who had been with us for about a year.

"Thank you for hiring my husband," she said.

I laughed. "Greg is a great contributor. We're happy to have him on the JMA team."

"You don't understand." She touched my arm. "He's truly happy at work. I love that his Sundays are no longer tainted because he didn't want to face Monday, and he's excited when Sunday evening approaches."

JMA adopted the motto GPTW—A Great Place to Work. Brian not only works in the business taking care of clients but also works on the business, constantly improving our culture of camaraderie and respect.

I continue my fervent prayer for JMA. No longer am I passionately crying out for God to smite our enemies and for our business to survive. Instead, I'm cheering from the sidelines as I pray the company grows into something more powerful than I ever imagined. I ask God to give everyone there His wisdom and clarity going forward. With Brian at the helm, I'm excited to see where JMA goes in the future.

About the Author

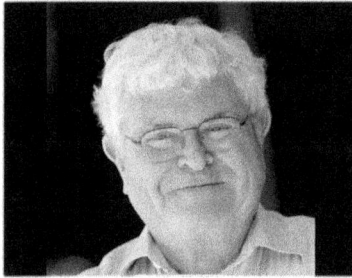

John Moore grew up with dreams of flying. As a teenager, he worked odd jobs in exchange for flying lessons from a friend from church. After receiving a scholarship through Air Force ROTC, John joined the United States Air Force (USAF), where he became a fighter pilot, graduated from the USAF Fighter Weapons School, and was selected to be the Weapons and Tactics officer for the first operational A-10 squadron.

The Air Force was also where John found his passion for finance, assisting his fellow pilots with their money management questions. He then discovered he could combine his love of finance with the joy he found in helping others. After military service, John dove headfirst into a career as a financial advisor in hopes of lifting others through his expertise.

John's commitment to his community and faith soon led him

to realize that he could better serve his clients by incorporating his faith values into his financial advice. Guiding his clients with biblical financial principles, he instilled the values of contentment and generosity. Driven to make a more profound impact, he founded John Moore Associates (JMA) in 1997 and later expanded with a second office in Arizona. He also co-founded Zia Trust, Inc. and serves as Zia's Board Chair.

John's influence extends beyond his business interests. He co-founded the Southwest Affiliate of the National Christian Foundation (www.ncfgiving.com) and continues to serve on its Board of Directors, striving to contribute to its growth and impact.

John is an engaged member of Arizona Charitable Gift Planners (www.azgiftplanners.org) and is proud to serve on the Advisory Board for the Colangelo College of Business at Grand Canyon University (www.gcu.edu).

As a Certified Kingdom Advisor®, John is committed to applying biblical wisdom in all areas of life and to the mission of Kingdom Advisors (www.kingdom advisors.com).

After handing off JMA's leadership to Brian Cochran, John has focused on encouraging generosity among those around him while spending time with his wife, Connie, and their family.

About Renown Publishing

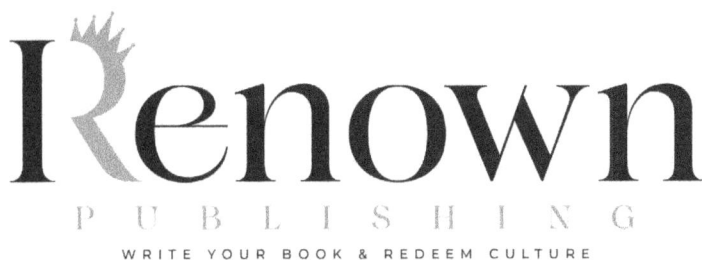

Renown Publishing is an elite team of professionals devoted to helping you shape, write, and share your book. Renown has written, edited, and worked on hundreds of books (including New York Times, Wall Street Journal, and USA Today best-sellers, and the #1 book on all of Amazon).

We believe authentic stories are the torch of change-makers, and our mission is to collaborate with purpose-driven authors to create societal impact and redeem culture.

If you're the founder of a purpose-driven company, or an aspiring author, visit RenownPublishing.com.